National Parks
Grand Teton

JOSH GREGORY

Children's Press®
An Imprint of Scholastic Inc.

Content Consultant
James Gramann, PhD
Professor, Department of Recreation, Park and Tourism Sciences
Texas A&M University, College Station, Texas

Library of Congress Cataloging-in-Publication Data
Names: Gregory, Josh, author.
Title: Grand Teton / by Josh Gregory.
Description: New York, NY : Children's Press, an imprint of Scholastic Inc., 2018. | Series: A true
    book | Includes bibliographical references and index.
Identifiers: LCCN 2017025794 | ISBN 9780531235072 (library binding) | ISBN 9780531238103 (pbk.)
Subjects: LCSH: Grand Teton National Park (Wyo.)—Juvenile literature.
Classification: LCC F767.T3 G84 2018 | DDC 978.7/55—dc23
LC record available at https://lccn.loc.gov/2017025794

All rights reserved. Published in 2018 by Children's Press, an imprint of Scholastic Inc.
Printed in Heshan, China   62

SCHOLASTIC, CHILDREN'S PRESS, A TRUE BOOK™, and associated logos are trademarks and/or
registered trademarks of Scholastic Inc.

Scholastic Inc., 557 Broadway, New York, NY 10012

1 2 3 4 5 6 7 8 9 10 R 27 26 25 24 23 22 21 20 19 18

**Front cover (main): The Tetons viewed
from the Christian Pond area**

Front cover (inset): A mountain biker

**Back cover: Rock climbers on
the Cloudveil Traverse**

Find the Truth!

Everything you are about to read is true *except* for one of the sentences on this page.

Which one is **TRUE**?

T or F Grand Teton National Park is home to the fastest mammal in North America.

T or F The park's glaciers have remained mostly unchanged in recent years.

Find the answers in this book.

Contents

THE BIG TRUTH!

National Parks Field Guide: Grand Teton

Mountain lion

4

Cascade Canyon

Bald eagle

A person canoes at Oxbow Bend in view of Mount Moran.

CHAPTER 1

The Beauty of the West

As you take in the view, you almost can't believe your eyes. A dramatic mountain range towers on the horizon. At the foot of the mountains, a colorful forest of tall trees stretches as far as you can see. All of this natural beauty is reflected in the crystal clear waters of the enormous lake in front of you. Grand Teton National Park is more breathtaking than you ever imagined.

Grand Teton
National Park

Valleys and Mountains

Grand Teton National Park covers about 485 square miles (1,256 square kilometers) of northwestern Wyoming. Millions of people travel here each year to experience the Teton Range of the Rocky Mountains. The jagged, rocky peaks pierce the sky thousands of feet above the valley floor. East of the range is Jackson Hole, a sprawling valley filled with lakes, rivers, forests, and great places to hike and camp.

A Timeline of Grand Teton National Park

About 9000 BCE

People arrive in the Teton area for the first time.

Early 1800s CE

Fur trappers come to the region in search of beaver furs.

Early 1900s

The region begins attracting tourists.

Early Explorers

The first people to explore the Teton Range and the surrounding area arrived about 11,000 years ago. They did not settle permanently in these mountains. The area, however, became an important source of food for Native Americans who made their homes nearby. These people included the Crow, the Nez Perce, the Shoshone, and many other groups. They hunted local animal species and collected plant foods such as berries and roots.

1929
U.S. Congress officially establishes Grand Teton National Park.

1950
The park is expanded to include much of Jackson Hole.

1972
The John D. Rockefeller Jr. Memorial Parkway opens, connecting Grand Teton National Park to Yellowstone National Park.

9

Setting Boundaries

In the 1800s, explorers from Europe and the United States began arriving in the Grand Teton area. They discovered that the region was packed with valuable resources, such as animals that could be hunted for their fur. Other people settled in Jackson Hole, where they started farms and ranches.

Just a few miles north of the Teton Range, Yellowstone National Park was established in 1872. Soon afterward, area residents began arguing that the Teton area should be added to Yellowstone. Instead, in 1929, Congress established Grand Teton National Park as a separate park. Twenty-one years later, the park's boundaries expanded to include Jackson Hole.

Beavers are a common sight in some parts of the park.

National Park Fact File

A national park is land that is protected by the federal government. It is a place of importance to the United States because of its beauty, history, or value to scientists. The U.S. Congress creates a national park by passing a law. Here are some key facts about Grand Teton National Park.

Grand Teton National Park	
Location	Northwestern Wyoming
Year established	1929
Size	About 310,000 acres (125,453 hectares)
Average number of visitors each year	3.3 million
Largest lake	Jackson Lake, at 15 miles (24 km) long and 7 miles (11 km) wide
Highest peak	Grand Teton, at 13,770 feet (4,197 meters)

Hikers along the park's many trails find stunning sights.

CHAPTER 2

From Valley to Mountaintop

It has taken a long time for Grand Teton National Park to become what it is today. The rock that forms the mountains of the Teton Range is roughly 2.7 billion years old. About 10 million years ago, this rock started shifting upward, just a few feet at a time, during a series of earthquakes. This process eventually formed the mountains as they are now.

The most recent major earthquake in the Teton Range occurred about 4,800 years ago.

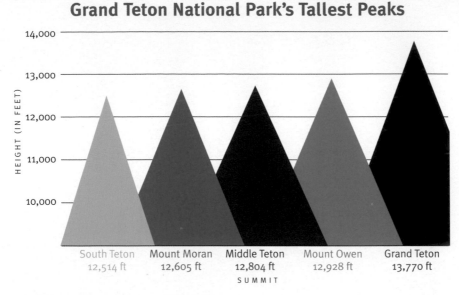

Grand Teton National Park's Tallest Peaks

HEIGHT (IN FEET)

14,000

13,000

12,000

11,000

10,000

South Teton
12,514 ft

Mount Moran
12,605 ft

Middle Teton
12,804 ft

Mount Owen
12,928 ft

Grand Teton
13,770 ft

SUMMIT

This graph compares the heights of some of the tallest peaks in the park.

The Park's Peaks

The Teton Range is made up of several towering mountain peaks. Eight of them stand more than 12,000 feet (3,658 m) high. The tallest is Grand Teton, at 13,770 feet (4,197 m).

Compared to other Rocky Mountain ranges and the Appalachian Mountains in eastern North America, the Teton Range formed fairly recently. This means its mountains have not had much time to become **eroded**. As a result, they have a sharp, jagged appearance.

Down in the Hole

Forests cover large parts of the mountainsides of the Teton Range. The trees extend down into the valley of Jackson Hole below. The park also contains a great deal of water. Lakes, rivers, and marshy wetlands can be found throughout Jackson Hole. **Glaciers** carved holes in the land and then melted, forming many of the area's lakes.

Fur trappers chose the name Jackson Hole because traveling down the steep mountainsides into the valley felt to them like climbing into a hole.

Hot and Cold

Visitors can experience a wide variety of weather. During summer, it is usually pleasant. Average high temperatures are nearly 80 degrees Fahrenheit (27 degrees Celsius) and it rains only occasionally. Winters can be harsh, however, with average lows in January of about 1 degree Fahrenheit (–17°C). Snow can pile up to more than 30 feet (9 m) high in the mountains.

For anyone who visits the park in winter, it's a good idea to wear warm, waterproof or water-resistant clothing.

Plenty to Do

The park's **diverse** landscape offers opportunities for all kinds of outdoor activities. There are more than 242 miles (389 km) of hiking trails to explore. Many visitors fish in the lakes and rivers or take a scenic bike ride. Experienced

Grand Teton National Park's lakes are a great place to kayak.

mountain climbers scale the park's highest peaks.

Camping and picnic areas are popular spots. Visitors with food, however, must be careful of bears. Park officials recommend storing food in bear-resistant containers to avoid attracting these dangerous animals.

CHAPTER 3

Animals Everywhere

Whether visitors are standing on the peak of Grand Teton, paddling a canoe across Jackson Lake, or exploring a wooded trail, they will see an incredible variety of creatures. With its varied landscape and **climate**, Grand Teton National Park is the perfect **habitat** for many animals. The chance to see these species in their natural homes is one of the park's greatest features.

Grizzly bears can run up to 30 miles per hour (48 kph) for short distances.

Grand Teton National Park is part of the pronghorn antelope's seasonal migration route. The U.S. government protects the entire 170-mile (274-km) pathway.

Marvelous Mammals

From small chipmunks and squirrels to enormous moose and grizzly bears, roughly 60 mammal species live throughout the park. Packs of wolves roam through forests. Campers might hear them howling at night. Mountain lions stalk **prey** high in the Teton Range. Visitors might glimpse a mountain goat hopping across ledges on a steep cliff. Beavers, otters, and other furry aquatic animals swim in lakes and rivers. In summer, visitors can look for the pronghorn antelope, the fastest North American mammal.

The Importance of Insects

They might be pesky sometimes, but insects play important roles in the park's **ecosystems**. Insects are food sources for larger animals, and many plants rely on the tiny creatures to reproduce. More than 10,000 insect species live within the boundaries of Grand Teton National Park. They range from bees that buzz through the air to shiny beetles that crawl along the ground. Visitors might even spot beautifully colored butterflies flitting from plant to plant.

At 3 inches (7.6 centimeters), long the park's calliope hummingbird is North America's smallest bird.

Up in the Air

Bird-watchers flock to Grand Teton National Park hoping to catch a glimpse of a rare species. More than 300 kinds of birds can be seen at different times of the year. Eagles, ospreys, and other predators circle the skies in search of prey below. Tiny hummingbirds zip from flower to flower, sipping **nectar** through their long beaks. Swans and other aquatic birds can be found around the park's waterways.

Crawling, Slithering, and Hopping

Grand Teton National Park is home to just four known reptile species. The only lizard is the northern sagebrush lizard. Visitors might see it in rocky areas. The other reptiles are all snakes. Don't worry, though. None of them are venomous!

The park is also home to a few amphibian species. There are four types of frogs, one kind of toad, and a single salamander species. These animals are found in wetter areas.

The first confirmed sighting of a northern sagebrush lizard in Grand Teton National Park was in 1992.

National Parks Field Guide: Grand Teton

Field guides have helped people identify wildlife and natural objects from birds to rocks for more than 100 years. Guides usually contain details about appearance, common locations, and other basics. Use this field guide to discover six animals you can spot in the park, and learn fascinating facts about each one!

Shiras moose

Scientific name: *Alces alces shirasi*

Habitat: Forested areas with nearby water sources

Diet: Fish, crustaceans

Fact: Weighing about 1,000 pounds (454 kilograms), the Shiras is the smallest of all moose subspecies.

Wandering garter snake

Scientific name: *Thamnophis elegans vagrans*

Habitat: Near rivers and lakes

Diet: A wide variety of small animals, including rodents, worms, fish, and frogs

Fact: This snake can release an unpleasant odor from its tail when it is trying to escape from danger.

Cutthroat trout

Scientific name: *Oncorhynchus clarkii*

Habitat: Rivers and lakes

Diet: Insects, smaller fish

Fact: A red marking under this trout's lower jaw makes it look like its throat was sliced, giving the fish its name.

Trumpeter swan

Scientific name: *Cygnus buccinator*

Habitat: Rivers, lakes, and ponds

Diet: Mostly aquatic plants

Fact: This huge bird gets its name from its unique, trumpetlike call.

Bald eagle

Scientific name: *Haliaeetus leucocephalus*

Habitat: Near water

Diet: Mostly fish, some other animals

Fact: Not only are these birds a U.S. symbol, they also build bigger nests than any other bird!

Yellow-bellied marmot

Scientific name: *Marmota flaviventris*

Habitat: Forests and rocky areas

Diet: Flowers, seeds, and grass

Fact: This rodent spends most of its time in underground burrows.

CHAPTER 4

The Park's Plants

From lush, green forests to meadows filled with colorful flowers, Grand Teton National Park has no shortage of places for plants to thrive. The more than 1,000 plant species provide homes and food sources for resident animals. Plants also give the park its beauty, with many species changing colors and appearance as the seasons change.

Visitors should not pick flowers in the park. Leave them for people and wildlife to enjoy!

A Trip Through the Trees

Growing high above most of the landscape, trees may be one of the first things you notice when entering the park. Most of the trees are **conifers**, which stay green all year. Some examples include the lodgepole pine, the Douglas fir, and the blue spruce.

In wetlands and near rivers, there are **deciduous** trees such as cottonwoods, aspens, and poplars. Their leaves turn beautiful shades of yellow and orange in the fall.

Close to the Ground

Visitors can also find plenty of plants by simply looking down at their feet. More than 100 types of grasses grow in the park, varying in height, color, and shape.

The park is also home to many shrubs. Especially common are sagebrush species. These short plants sprout from rocky soil and cover huge areas of Jackson Hole.

Short, sturdy sagebrush plants are common across the valley.

Unexpected and Beautiful Blooms

Looking closely at tree trunks, rocks, and other surfaces, a person can see smaller forms of life. Mosses are tiny plants that grow in clumps, forming a carpet-like green coating. They do not need soil to grow. They are found where other plants are uncommon, such as high rocky areas.

Many of the park's plants produce colorful flowers. Different plants bloom at different times between May and September. This means the park is constantly changing color during the warmer months. The types of flowers also vary across the park. The biggest, most impressive blooms grow in forests and the sagebrush-covered areas of Jackson Hole. These range from red gilias to sunflowers. Smaller flowers such as the alpine forget-me-not grow higher up on the mountainsides.

Alpine

Short, hardy shrubs and flowers that can survive the dry and windy conditions grow highest in the mountains.

Alpine forget-me-not

Sky pilot

Canyons and Slopes

Conifer forests of firs, pines, and spruces are mixed with meadows of grasses and wildflowers. Trees become sparser higher up.

Mountain ash

Douglas fir

Valleys

Shrubs, wildflowers, and grasses flourish. Deciduous trees grow near waterways. Some conifers are also found here.

Cottonwood

Sagebrush

CHAPTER 5

Fighting for the Future

One of a national park's most important purposes is to protect its land and the many things that live there. This is becoming more of a challenge for the scientists, rangers, and other people who keep the park safe. These experts must search for ways to limit the damage done by human activities.

 Each winter, Grand Teton National Park rangers broadcast shows from a desk made of snow!

Roads and fences cause problems for migrating elk, antelopes, and other park animals.

A Changing World

Climate change is one of the biggest issues facing the environment. The burning of fossil fuels and other human activities release gases that trap heat in Earth's atmosphere. This changes weather patterns and increases temperatures all over the world. Some Grand Teton wildlife, such as pikas and moose, are especially at risk from climate change. These creatures cannot tolerate warmer temperatures. They may one day disappear from the park completely.

Scientists track the effects of climate change in the park. One way they do this is by observing the glaciers that lie in the mountains. These huge chunks of ice have been melting much faster than usual in recent years. Some experts predict that the smaller glaciers could disappear within decades. Because glaciers are an important source of water in parts of the park, this could cause problems for wildlife.

Melted ice from the Schoolroom Glacier forms a small lake. The lake is turquoise because of the minerals in the water.

Invasive Species

Not all of the life in the park came to the area by natural means. Human travelers brought some plants and animals into the park, often without realizing it. One example is the New Zealand mud snail. These invasive species can cause big problems for native wildlife. They may take space and food away from native species and can spread quickly. Park workers sometimes fight invasive plants using chemicals. They also destroy them by hand, or release insects to help get rid of them.

New Zealand mud snails are tiny, but they can cause serious problems, such as competing with native snails for food.

Kids Helping Out

To continue protecting the park, young people will have to pick up where other park workers leave off. Grand Teton National Park has multiple ways for kids to get involved. The Youth **Conservation** Program has teens work there each summer for a firsthand look at park preservation. The Pura Vida program focuses on Latino teens. Part of the program involves service projects such as patrolling trails and identifying invasive species. The teens also learn canoeing, cross-country skiing, and other sports.

Friendly Flames

It might seem surprising, but one way park workers keep the environment healthy is by setting it on fire. Wildfires have occurred naturally in the park since long before humans arrived in the area. The burning improves the soil quality, clears out dead plant material, and helps many types of plants grow. Today, park workers set carefully controlled fires in sections of the park as they are needed.

A specialist keeps a close eye on a fire to make sure it stays under control.

Keeping Watch

The first step in protecting the park is simply keeping an eye on everything happening there. Park workers try to spot warning signs early. This can give them a chance to save a species from **extinction** or prevent

A scientist holds a baby mountain lion captured in Grand Teton National Park.

environmental damage. The Greater Yellowstone Network (GRYN) keeps track of local wildlife, conducts tests on soil and water, and performs other tasks. The data helps park staff ensure the park will remain as it is for years to come. ★

Map Mystery

One of Grand Teton National Park's many incredible landmarks is a log cabin. The cabin was built there in the 1880s. What is it called? Follow the directions to find the answer.

Directions

1. Start at the park's southern entrance.

2. Head north past the airport to a junction named after a huge, hooved animal.

3. Take the northeast path to a turnout point where you can gaze at the three huge Teton mountains.

4. Travel northwest to the first big lake you find.

5. Head northeast and you'll reach your destination.

GRAND TETON NATIONAL PARK

Flagg Ranch Information Center

Colter Bay Visitor Center

Jenny Lake Visitor Center

Cunningham Cabin Historic Site

Teton Point Turnout

Moose Junction

Park Headquarters

Jackson Hole Airport

Craig Thomas Discovery and Visitor Center

Park Entrance (south)

Jackson Lake

Leigh Lake

Jenny Lake

Mount Moran

Mount Owen

Grand Teton

Middle Teton

South Teton

Phelps Lake

Snake River

RANGE

TETON

JACKSON HOLE

U.S.
Area of map

Alaska and Hawai'i are not drawn to scale or placed in their proper places.

Compass Rose

North

West — East

South

Answer: Cuningham Cabin Historic Site

Be an Animal Tracker!

If you're ever in Grand Teton National Park, keep an eye out for these animal tracks. They'll help you know which animals are in the area.

Moose
Hoof length: 6 inches (15.2 cm)

Grizzly bear
Paw length: 6 inches (15.2 cm)

Black bear
Paw length: 4.5 inches (11.4 cm)

Mountain lion
Paw length: 3 inches (7.6 cm)

Wolf
Paw length: 5 inches (12.7 cm)

Bison
Hoof length: 5 inches (12.7 cm)

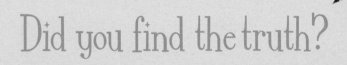

True Statistics

Total length of trails in the park: 242 mi. (389 km)

Number of mountains above 12,000 ft. (3,658 m) in elevation: 8

Number of lakes in the park: More than 100

Number of fish species in the park: 16

Number of mammal species: About 60

Number of reptile species: 4

Number of amphibian species: 6

Number of insect species: More than 10,000

Number of bird species: More than 300

Number of plant species: More than 1,000

Did you find the truth?

T Grand Teton National Park is home to the fastest mammal in North America.

F The park's glaciers have remained mostly unchanged in recent years.

Resources

Books

Flynn, Sarah Wassner, and Julie Beer. *National Parks Guide U.S.A.*
  Washington, DC: National Geographic, 2016.

Prentzas, G. S. *Wyoming*. New York: Children's Press, 2015.

Wallace, Audra. *Yellowstone*. New York: Children's Press, 2018.

Visit this Scholastic website for more information on Grand Teton National Park:
★ www.factsfornow.scholastic.com
Enter the keywords **Grand Teton**

Important Words

climate (KLYE-mit) the weather typical of a place over a long period of time

conifers (KAH-nuh-furz) evergreen trees that produce their seeds in cones

conservation (kahn-sur-VAY-shuhn) the protection of valuable resources, especially forests, wildlife, natural resources, or artistic or historic objects

deciduous (de-SIJ-oo-uhs) shedding all leaves every year in the fall

diverse (di-VURS) having many different types or kinds

ecosystems (EE-koh-sis-tuhmz) all the living things in certain places and their relation to their environment

eroded (i-ROHD-id) worn away gradually by water or wind

extinction (ik-STINGKT-shuhn) the state of no longer being found alive

glaciers (GLAY-shurz) slow-moving masses of ice found in mountain valleys or polar regions

habitat (HAB-i-tat) the place where an animal or plant is usually found

nectar (NEK-tur) a sweet liquid from flowers

prey (PRAY) an animal that is hunted by another animal for food

Index

Page numbers in **bold** indicate illustrations.

About the Author

Josh Gregory is the author of more than 100 books for kids. He has written about everything from animals to technology to history. A graduate of the University of Missouri-Columbia, he currently lives in Portland, Oregon.